Victoria May
19 Sandwell mansions
Wednesday.
for

Helen Exley Giftbooks
for the most thoughtful gifts of all

OTHER BOOKS IN THIS SERIES:

For a wonderful Grandmother A book to make your own
For a real Friend A book to make your own
A Girl's Journal A personal notebook and keepsake
A Woman's Journal A personal notebook and keepsake
Cats A book to make your own
Teddy Bears A book to make your own
Inspirations A book to make your own
A Gardener's Journal A book to make your own

OTHER HELEN EXLEY GIFTBOOKS
FOR MOTHERS:

The Love Between Mothers and Daughters
To a very special Mother
To the World's best Mother (a book by kids)
A Little Book for my Mother

Published in hardback 1990. Published in softcover 2001.

12 11 10 9 8 7 6 5 4

ISBN 1-86187-184-8

Selection and design by Helen Exley
Illustrated by Juliette Clarke
Printed in China

Helen Exley Giftbooks, 16 Chalk Hill, Watford, Herts, WD19 4BG, UK.
Helen Exley Giftbooks LLC, 185 Main Street, Spencer, MA 01562, USA.
www.helenexleygiftbooks.com

For a wonderful Mother

A BOOK TO MAKE YOUR OWN

A HELEN EXLEY GIFTBOOK

With the approach of Mother's Day, the mob of wild-eyed daughters progressing from shop to shop are all looking for cards that just say "Thanks, mom. I love you".

PETER GRAY

To my mam

My proudest pleasure is
when my beautiful little
three-year-old girl puts
her arms around my neck, she
squeezes me tight and says
"I love you mummy, I really do."

A. COOPER

A MOTHER UNDERSTANDS
WHAT A CHILD DOES NOT SAY.

JEWISH PROVERB

Mums are inclined to go out into the kitchen to make a pot of tea when the News repeats the story of the missing child, the famine, the earthquake. She is all those other mothers. And she is powerless.

PAM BROWN

Every man, for the sake of the great blessed Mother in Heaven,
and for the love of his own little mother on earth,
should handle all womankind gently, and hold them in all honour.

ALFRED LORD TENNYSON

I shall never forget my mother, for it was she who planted and nurtured the first seeds of good within me. She opened my heart to the impressions of nature; she awakened my understanding and extended my horizon, and her precepts exerted an everlasting influence upon the course of my life.

IMMANUEL KANT

Mothers are inclined
to feel limp at fifty.
This is because the children
have taken most of her stuffing
to build their nests.

SAMANTHA ARMSTRONG

MUMS ARE NOT SO MUCH CONCERNED
ABOUT EDUCATION, PAEDIATRICS, CHILD POVERTY,
LAW AND ORDER AND THE ARMS RACE
AS ABOUT EMILY AND ROBERT AND IMRAM AND NJOROGE.
WHICH IS, AFTER ALL, THE SAME THING.

CLARE D'ARCY

Sometimes, unexpectedly, you'll hear them say something with firm conviction – and they are your words and it is your voice. Echoing down the years from a day half forgotten – a day of non-event, a day lost among other days. Children take what they need from us – not what we offer.

PAM BROWN

*She is my first, great love. She was a wonderful,
rare woman – you do not know; as strong, and steadfast,
and generous as the sun. She could be as swift
as a white whiplash, and as kind and gentle as warm rain,
and as steadfast as the irreducible earth beneath us.*

D.H. LAWRENCE

... in motherhood the woman
discovers another kind of loving,
for however time or circumstance
may come between her and her child,
their lives are interwoven forever.
Willingly or unwillingly
she has projected herself forward
into Time, and will from now on,
see the world through other eyes
than her own.

PAM BROWN

Some are kissing mothers
and some are scolding mothers,
but it is love just the same,
and most mothers kiss and scold together.

PEARL BUCK

A MOTHER IS A WOMAN
WITH A TWENTY-FIVE HOUR DAY WHO CAN STILL
FIND AN HOUR TO PLAY WITH HER FAMILY.

IRIS PECK

1964
ON
½ cm

Giving advice comes naturally to mothers.

Advice is in the genes along with blue eyes and red hair.

LOIS WYSE

Inside every elderly human being
is a small child missing its mom.

HELEN THOMSON

I can find no words to explain how motherhood succeeded in changing me. I who prided myself on being a sophisticated intellectual, with no interest in babies and a strong determination never to sink into domesticity, was transported into a world in which my children are the most vital part of my whole existence.

YETTA PETERSON

Kindness is contagious. . . . One truly affectionate soul in a family will exert a sweetening and harmonizing influence upon all its members. . . . Beginning with the highest, the ointment drops even upon those who are unconscious or careless of it, and the whole house is presently filled with its fragrance.

HENRY VAN DYKE

PEOPLE ADMIRE ME FOR MY ACHIEVEMENTS
AS A BUSINESS WOMAN.
I KNOW THAT MY GREATEST ACHIEVEMENT
WAS BEING AN ORDINARY MOM.

HELEN EXLEY

I can't imagine what was so special about being a couple; being a family is so much nicer.

ALISON McWILLIAMS

Dearest Mother
Victoria Cottage
21 May.

My dear Mother, the growth of a lifetime
is not cut down by absence. . . let me tell you
as earnestly and gladly as I can, that I never loved you
so devotedly as I do this moment. . . .
That in my happiest hours, my happiness
has been incomplete without you.

EDMUND CLARENCE STEDMAN

J.A.M.
Homemade
Blackberry.
Homemade
Blackberry
Jam

Home made jam from mom
is really bottled love.

H.M.E.

Mums know whose turn it is to have the skin off the rice pudding, whose turn it is to lick out the cake mixbowl. They know when it's a real stomach ache and when it's physics morning. They know the difference between a bit of fantasizing and a straight lie; between heat rash and measles; between "I Must Have" and "I Want". Solomon was an amateur.

PAM BROWN

Mothers know when they
are being given a treat – they can hear
the fight going on in the kitchen.

PETER GRAY

*If evolution really works,
how come mothers have only
two hands?*

ED DUSSAULT

A CHINESE PROVERB
TELLS US THAT
"A HUNDRED MEN
MAY MAKE AN ENCAMPMENT,
BUT IT TAKES A WOMAN
TO MAKE A HOME".

A.J. BUCKNALL

Mothers taken to the theatre
when the kids are tiny, phone the baby sitter in the
interval to see if they are alive and happy.
Mothers taken to the theatre when the kids are in
their teens phone home in the interval to see
if it's still standing.

PETER GRAY

Nothing looks as lonely as your mom
before she sees you coming up the platform.

PAM BROWN

Mothers need transfusions fairly often –
phone calls, letters, bright postcards from
the Outer Hebrides.

HEULWEN ROBERTS

THE EVERLASTING SADNESS OF ANY MOTHER
IS THAT THERE COMES A TIME
WHEN SHE CAN NO LONGER BRING MAGIC TO YOUR LIFE,
NOR CURE YOUR TROUBLES.

DIANA BRISCOE

It doesn't matter how old I get,
whenever I see anything new or splendid,
I want to call "Mum, come and look".

HELEN THOMSON

My mom is a lady who has had a lot of problems in her life. Most of them me. . . .

DIANA BRISCOE

Never tell your kids how well you did at school.
Mum still has your reports.

ITOKO FUJITA

No matter how old a mother is,
she watches her middle-aged children for signs of improvement.

FLORIDA SCOTT-MAXWELL

The trouble with mothers is that however well groomed and sophisticated you appear to strangers, they know your knickers are probably held up with a safety pin.

SAMANTHA ARMSTRONG

Fifty-four years of love and tenderness and crossness and devotion and unswerving loyalty. Without her I could only have achieved a quarter of what I have achieved, not only in terms of success and career, but in terms of personal happiness. . . . She has never stood between me and my life, never tried to hold me too tightly, always let me go free. . . .

NOEL COWARD, ABOUT HIS MOTHER

The more I reflect on the situation of the mother, the more I am struck with the extent of her powers, and the inestimable values of her services. In the language of love, women are called angels; but this is a weak and silly compliment; they approach nearer to our idea of the Deity: they not only create, but sustain their creation, and hold its future destiny in their hands, every man is what his mother made him, and to her he must be indebted for the greatest blessings in life. . . .

WILLIAM BUCHAN

A mother and her daughter grow closer every time they have a successful shopping spree. Shoes off, kettle on, loot divided. It dates back to the Cave....

SAMANTHA ARMSTRONG

One's mom is, to a large extent, a product of one's own imagination – that is why it is so unnerving when they behave like themselves.

ROBERT E. JUDD

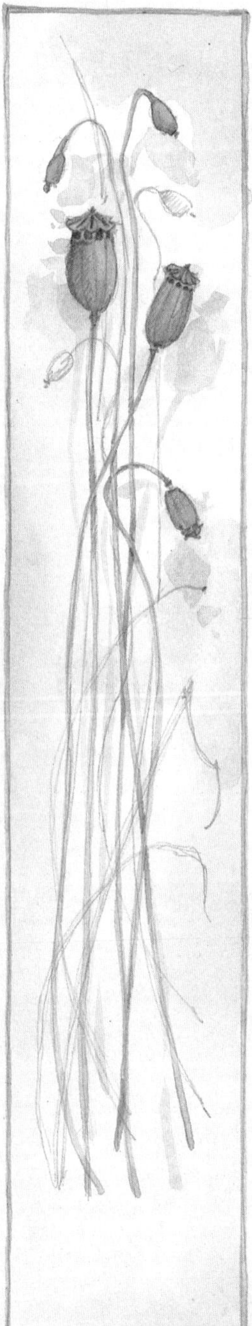

BECAUSE SHE IS A MOTHER

She broke the bread into two fragments and gave them to the children, who ate with avidity.
"She hath kept none for herself," grumbled the Sergeant.
"Because she is not hungry," said a soldier
"because she is a mother," said the Sergeant.

VICTOR HUGO

WHETHER YOU LIKE IT OR NOT, YOUR MOTHER GOES WITH YOU. FOREVER.

HELEN EXLEY

All mothers are rich when they love their children.
There are no poor mothers, no ugly ones, no old ones.
Their love is always the most beautiful of the joys.
And when they seem most sad, it needs but a kiss which
they receive or give to turn all their tears into stars. . . .

MAURICE MAETERLINCK

. . . we are still no further away than we ever were
and when the pain to see you comes, I don't let it hurt
and I don't kill it either for it is the sweetest pain I feel.
If sons will go off and marry, or be war correspondents,
or managers, it doesn't mean that Home
is any less Home. . . .

RICHARD HARDING DAVIS, FROM A LETTER TO HIS MOTHER

. . . YOU WILL NEVER KNOW
HOW MUCH I LOVE YOU
ALL AND YOU MUST NEVER GIVE UP
TRYING TO COMPREHEND IT.
GOD BLESS YOU AND KEEP YOU,
AND MY LOVE TO YOU EVERY MINUTE
AND ALWAYS.

RICHARD HARDING DAVIS,
FROM A LETTER TO HIS MOTHER

Darling ma
Than
your letter, and
marys Gardens
uary 23